Celtic Illumination

The Irish School

Border decoration from the Macdurnan Gospels, 9th century

ex libris

Above: St Mark, St Gall Gospel Book, 8th century
Opposite: St Mark, Macdurnan Gospels, 9th century

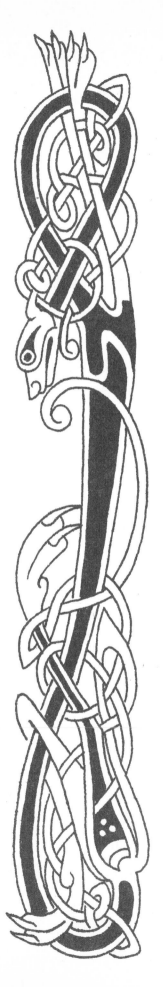
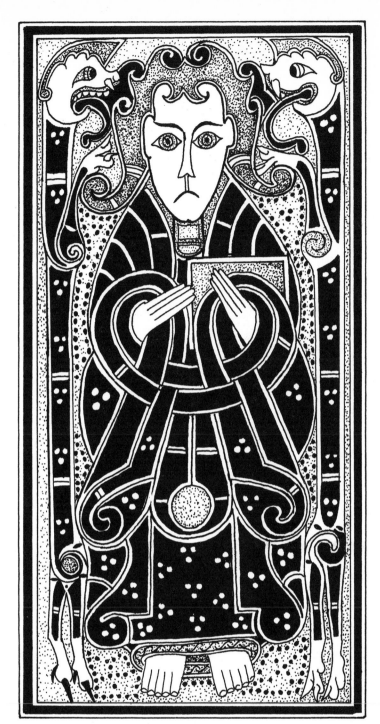

CELTIC ILLUMINATION

The Irish School

Courtney Davis

With 106 illustrations, 8 in color

THAMES AND HUDSON

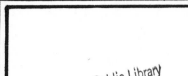

Artwork and text copyright © 1998 Courtney Davis

First published in the United States of America in 1998 by Thames and Hudson Inc., 500 Fifth Avenue, New York, New York 10110

Library of Congress Catalog Card Number 97-61610
ISBN 0-500-28039-8

Printed and bound in Slovenia

Border from the Macdurnan Gospels, 9th century

Courtney Davis has created over twenty-eight books since he began working in 1977, and is one of the most celebrated artists in the field of Celtic art. He has exhibited his paintings in cathedrals, churches and galleries in Britain, as well as in Continental Europe and the United States. He lives and works from his studio in Abbotsbury, Dorset.

An adaptation of the portrait of St John, Book of Kells, 9th century

5

Dedicated to St Columba on the 1400th anniversary of his death, and in my twentieth year as a Celtic artist, my grateful thanks to those scribes who have guided my hand.

My special thanks to Dimity, Blaine and Bridie for their support.

Panel from the Book of Kells, 9th century

Contents

Detail from the Macregol Gospels, 9th century

Initials from the Corpus Missal, 12th century

St Luke, Macdurnan Gospels, 9th century

Introduction

Celtic Christian Illumination

In addition to its being a glorious testimony to human ingenuity, skill and imagination, one of the most striking things about Celtic Christian illumination is its power to hold a viewer's attention, compelling one to pause and study its details. It can soon make one contemplative. As the eye follows intricate patterns and the mind teases the most casual observer with the question, 'How could any hand ever have done this?', the viewer is already drawn into an entirely other world – a world where the spirit is nurtured and the person enlightened.

This communion with the other world and the beings who populate it is what Eastern Christians seek when they gaze into the eyes of an icon of Christ, of his Mother, or of one of the other saints. It is what people have sought from time immemorial when turning to shamans for assistance in making other world journeys.

In the ancient Celtic past, artists emerged who had the shamanic ability to seize people's imaginations and draw them into subliminal experiences of superhuman power in loving, creating, and even destroying. The touch of those who had this skill can still be discerned in the compelling labyrinthine designs which grace Celtic manuscripts. This is the expansive power of the bards, and it still has the power to transform us.

In the pre-Christian Celtic world, Druidic, or bardic, schools trained those who would *become* the living memory of the people. While the druids kept folk memory alive through ritual, the bards did so through the recounting of stories and history. It took twenty years before a person was considered fully trained and initiated, either as a druid or as a bard. A major reason is that everything had to be memorized perfectly. It is not that the bards were illiterate – there is ample evidence that they were as literate and well educated as any of their Greek or Roman counterparts – but the remembering of Celtic history and of the details of religious observance was considered such a sacred matter that the possibility of eventual scribal error or the risk of anything similar to the colossal loss the ancient world suffered with the burning of the great Library of Alexandria had to be avoided.

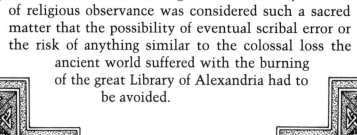

Corners from the Macdurnan Gospels, 9th century

Crucifixion from the Book of Dimma, 8th century

During the initial period of Ireland's Christianization, monastic institutions flourished along with the older Druidic establishments, but as Druidism began to fade during the Christian centuries, the older Druidic skills were carried out by the bards, many of whom also became monks. A number of the early abbots and abbesses received both kinds of training.

As the bardic institutions had committed the totality of their learning to human memories, so the Christian institutions gathered all the written literature they could into their libraries. As a legacy for future generations, they preserved and reproduced these treasures by hand. In doing this strenuous, meticulous work they were rendering the world a service similar to the work done in other European monasteries. The one ingredient which made a vast difference was that the monks who produced the Irish Gospel Books had bardic imaginations. From their Druidic and bardic forebears they inherited an almost superstitious awe of the power of words. They knew about the effects of verbal spells cast by the druids, and they knew the power of the bards – not only to remember every word of a story with perfect precision and to tell it flawlessly, but also to make the story come alive through the imaginative way it was narrated with brilliant verbal embellishment and accompanying music. Such performances could mesmerize and transport entire audiences to other times and places.

For Christian monks, there was no text more sacred than the Bible. So with bardic meticulousness they tried to copy every word. They knew the Gospel to be the living Word of God because of the power it retained to transform people's lives, so they breathed soul into the pages of the sacred text by filling every bit of space with riots of colour and splendid intricacies of design encompassing design and framed by more design. A page might have only a single word of text – perhaps merely a capital letter – but it would be alive with decorative flourishes, blended with minuscule stylized people, animals, angels, mythological creatures, and other bits of pure scribal whimsy.

In rabbinic tradition all sacred scripture is the inspired Word of God – even the part of each page which is not covered by the individual letters and words. In addition to using the sacred text to touch our minds, God uses the in-between spaces to engage our imaginations and reach our hearts. It is the space between the letters that encourages us to move beyond rigid observance of religious precepts into genuine communion with life-enhancing, freedom-giving divine spirit.

Celtic Christians were so convinced of the sacredness and healing power of the books that they would sometimes lower them into wells to bless the

water and transfer to it some of the healing energy. They were sure that no harm would come to such books. While some of the codices which have survived do, alas, show evidence of water damage, I have seen Courtney Davis demonstrate the way that gazing at Celtic art can increase a person's energy and bring healing to the spirit.

Today we cannot imagine how vital these books were to their creators and to those who held them in sacred trust. Some saints would even violate the law to retain such books. Impetuous young St Columba caused the first copyright controversy in history by copying St Finnian's cherished manuscript, 'St Martin's Gospel', without permission and then refusing to return it, even when ordered to do so by King Diarmuid. This codex, known as the Cathach of St Columba, was used as a sacred palladium, protecting the members of the O'Donnell clan, who carried it with them into battle.

There are many today who yearn for a sense of being on track with the not yet realized goal of their life's pilgrimage. They seek to transcend whatever is trivial or spiritually damaging and nurture their spirits from the fonts of pure wisdom and divine life – for them and for all who seek beauty, truth, and a taste of the other world, Courtney Davis' tribute to the Irish Gospel Books should provide a feast indeed.

Father Dennis O'Neill
St Benedict Rectory
Chicago
January 1997

Panel from the Book of Durrow, 7th century

Early Christian Ireland

Christianity was introduced into Ireland in the early 5th century. Although not all the Irish kings accepted Christianity from Patrick, including Loguire the High King who remained pagan, there was little opposition to this new faith and Patrick was permitted to continue his ministry and to move freely throughout Ireland, baptizing the converts and ordaining the clergy for the new churches that he founded. Each church was within a circular enclosure based on the triple ramparted ring fort or crannog, which surrounded a dwelling house for the clerics, the kitchen/refectory and the church itself. These churches established by Patrick were not monastic – although the bishops governed the centres known as 'cities', there is only one mention of a bishop being handed a church. In 444 St Patrick founded the Monastery of Armagh – the first to be founded and the most important. In the early 9th century, texts relating to St Patrick were copied into a volume which is now known as the Book of Armagh.

In 4th- and 5th-century Egypt Christians had became weary of the fearful temptations of the great cities such as Alexandria and began to flock to the deserts and barren mountains. They followed the example of Saints Paul

Detail from the Book of Kells, 8th century

and Anthony and became hermits and monks seeking spiritual perfection through solitude, penance and fasting. This ascetic monasticism originated from Syria, Egypt and Palestine, the birthplace of Christianity, and began to appear in Britain in the 5th century – many simple living communities were set up in the most desolate and remote places, superseding the episcopal form of Christianity.

Cut off from the centres of Christendom by the barbarian invasions, 5th-century Ireland became influenced by the Western British church through the missionaries who came to their shores. Also, many Irishmen travelled to Britain and went to study at the monasteries in, for instance, Candida Casa (Whithorn) in Galloway and Mynyw (St David's) in Wales.

David and Goliath, Cotton MS Vitellius F.XI, 10th century

St Enda, who returned to Ireland after his studies at Candida Casa, was granted the three Aran Islands in 490 by the King of Munster to set up, with 150 followers, a small Christian settlement of beehive stone cells on what was no more than broad shelves of rock rising 300 feet out of the battering Atlantic Ocean. Under a rule of great severity, the character of the Irish Church was formed. Many Irish monks and hermits who had studied in Britain returned to Ireland in search of secluded places to build cells in which they could live their lives of prayer and fasting. Many followers of these holy men arrived and small communities were formed around them.

By the end of the 5th century, Armagh, the primatial see, had become monastic and St Brigit had founded her great community for monks and the 'Virgins of Christ' at Kildare. All the scribes known to us are male, yet it is possible that some of the books were illuminated by the nuns. Monastic centres stretched across Ireland – at Seir, Clonmacnois, Derry, Durrow, Bangor, Nendrum, Glendalough, and in many other places. St Finnian, under the influence of Cadoc of Llancarvan in South Wales, transformed the Patrician Church of Clonard into a monastery which rapidly grew with great renown. The ecclesiastical organization established by Patrick had begun to wither away by this time: now the scattered monasteries across the country followed the rule of their founders.

Unlike the Desert Fathers, the Irish monasticism movement valued letters and learning and the need to spread the Christian message through their missionary work. The Irish missionaries made many converts through example, mainly because they did not seek worldly goods or temporal power – they preached only by their practice.

By the 6th century, the well-organized and less ascetic Benedictine order gradually began to take over the Irish monasteries one by one. The monks in Ireland started to acquire corporate wealth through donations of land and churches to their monasteries. This gradual corruption led to a movement of spiritual reform within the monasteries. Known as the Céle Dé (servants of God), they were especially active in the south and east – their main centres were at Finglas and Tallaght. They laid great stress on the study and perfection of the Liturgy and meditation. In the 8th century Finglas and Tallaght were to be among the first to suffer attack by the Viking raiders who destroyed most of the Gospel Books to retrieve the precious stones and gold from their covers.

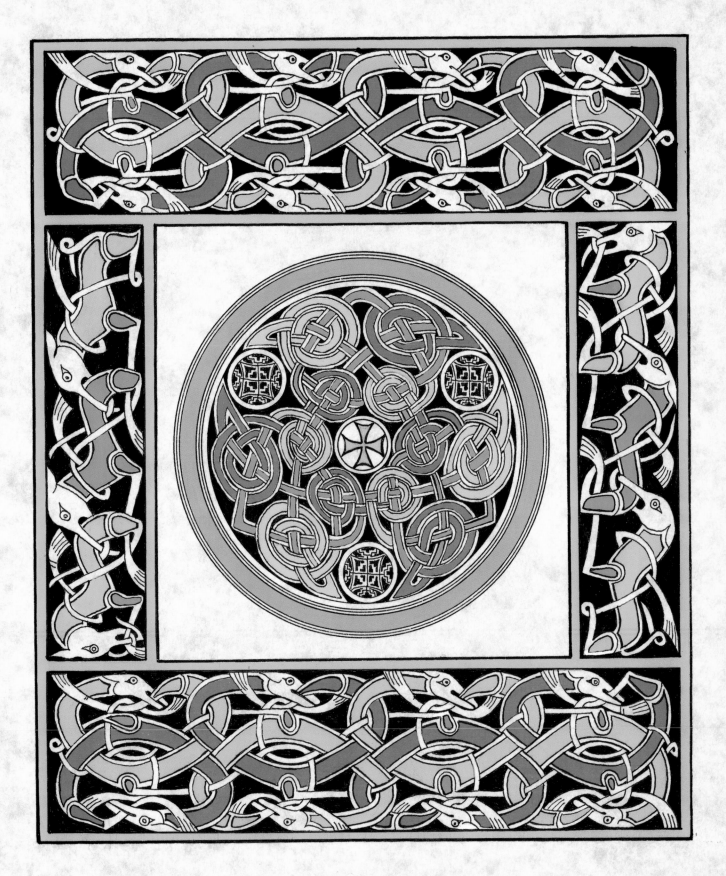

Plate I

Plate II

Plate III

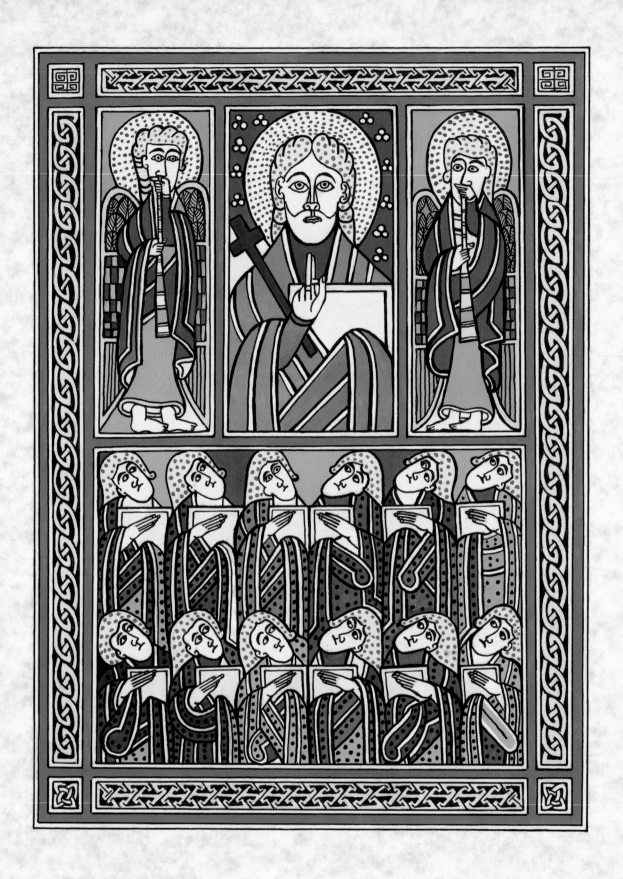

Plate IV

Plate V

Plate VI

Plate VII

uen nat; 2
dat; 2 nob
in hum eñ d
no 2 magm
Multiplicab
oncede qm̄
dr̄:uiniorum
noua p̄carnē
liberet qr̄ ru
1ugo uet; tarh
R̄es; multifa
rie multiph
olim dr̄loq
bz mpplūr.
āu diebz iy

Plate VIII

Colour plates

The Early Celtic Manuscripts

The earliest surviving Irish manuscript is known as the Codex Usserianus Primus, which was produced around 600. This early specimen of Irish script is a sadly mutilated copy of the pre-Jerome version of the Gospels, the earliest example of an Insular artist copying a Mediterranean form of decoration. Its ornament is confined to linear and dot patterns in the colophons, and it confirms that Celtic book decoration had not yet acquired a distinct character of its own. The Cathach of St Columba, thought to have been written between 591 and 597, followed. Tradition tells us that it was written by Columba himself and that it is the copy he took from the book lent to him by St Finnian, which led to an argument over who owned it and to Columba's departure from Ireland. The scribes' ornamentation is a tentative but distinct decoration consisting of the same weak scrolls that also appear on hat pins and brooches of that period. The initials are drawn with the same red and brown inks as the script.

By the 7th century the monasteries of Ireland became not only centres of prayer and penance, but also of learning; there is an abundance of evidence that Latin was studied, though only a little for Greek. St Columbanus, an

Initial from the Cathach of St Columba, 7th century

exceptional man, was a product of the Irish schools and he later founded a series of monasteries on the Continent. His writings show us that he was well acquainted with the works of Virgil, Horace, Ovid, Gildas and Gregory the Great, as well as the scriptures. He wrote prose and verse in excellent Latin, and dealt confidently with questions of philosophy and theology.

Though modest in comparison with the learning of later medieval Europe, the level of teaching given by the Irish monks was high by contemporary Western standards. The students scratched their lessons on wax tablets using a stylus, while the more skilled copied or illuminated manuscripts in the scriptorium. Great care was taken transcribing Gospel Books which were to be used on the altar. Books on the lives of the saints, astronomy and natural history were also copied or compiled by the monks. Several features of the early Irish books show that much of the Irish scribes' early inspiration came in part from Coptic scriptoria, especially in the dot contouring and the way that the pages are gathered.

The eagle, symbol of St John, Book of Durrow, 7th century

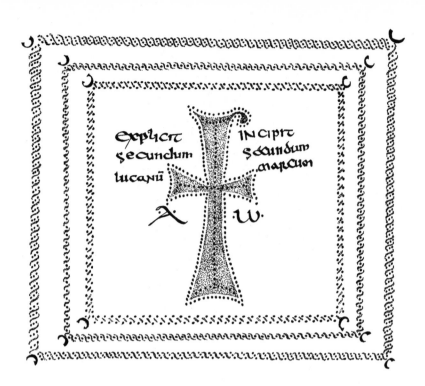

Gospel Book Codex Usserianus Primus
Trinity College Library, Dublin, MS A.4.15

The Codex Usserianus Primus was written around 600 and is probably one of the earliest specimens of Irish script. The Celtic scribe at this time had not acquired the distinct character of later Celtic book decoration and the Codex is an early example of an Irish scribe copying a Mediterranean form of decoration. Its leaves are badly damaged and discoloured. The only remaining decoration is the Xp monogram in reddish brown, with the *explicit* of Luke and the *incipit* of Mark written on either side. The red dotting around and within the cross is similar to the book ornament that was to follow and is also accompanied by the Greek letters 'a' and 'w', alpha and omega.

The book is named after James Ussher, Archbishop of Armagh, who died in 1576, but it is not thought to have been owned by him. The Codex Usserianus Primus was enclosed in a *cumdach* (shrine).

Reconstruction of the damaged Xp monogram page from the Codex Usserianus Primus, early 7th century

Cathach of St Columba
MS S.N. Royal Irish Academy, Dublin

The Cathach is traditionally identified as being a copy made by St Columba the Elder, who died in 597, of a book lent to him by St Finnian – this led to a dispute over the ownership of the copied book, following which Columba left Ireland and founded the monastic settlement on Iona in Scotland. The Cathach was probably written between 591 and 597 and is the earliest Irish Psalter (book of Psalms) extant.

The text and illumination were the work of one scribe, although it is unlikely that it was Columba. The scribe who invented the initials in the Cathach may not have been a great artist but he did take an extremely important step in a new direction. Each of the sixty-four Psalms within the psalter has its own initial in black ink with a simple decoration in the form of trumpets, spirals which are linked to the lingering tradition of Celtic La Tène art and guilloch patterns (an ornamental band or border with repeating pattern of two or more wavy lines). The initials are often outlined with red lead dots. The closing motif is often a spiral line, though sometimes it is replaced by a gaping animal head, fish or a porpoise.

The Cathach (which means battler) was taken into battle as a talisman to ensure victory.

The book was discovered in 1813 when the shrine in which it was contained was opened.

Initial from the Cathach of St Columba, 591–97

Antiphonary of Bangor
MS C.5.INF. Biblioteca Ambrosiana, Milan

The Antiphonary of Bangor is the earliest extant manuscript written in Irish minuscule. It is a collection of religious hymns and poems, two of which connect this codex with the monastery of Bangor on the southern shore of Belfast Lough in Downpatrick. It was founded in 517 by St Comgall, one of the most famous of the earlier Irish saints, who became the first abbot of the monastery and died there in 602 at the age of eighty-five. The Antiphonary was produced in Bangor between around 680 and 691, escaping destruction at the hands of the Danes, who for about two centuries from 795 onwards ravaged and pillaged the northern part of Ireland. They were said to have had a special animosity against books, burning them and throwing them into the water. Bangor was more than once wasted and plundered by the Danes. In 824 we are told that the shrine of St Comgall was smashed, with its learned men and bishops put to the sword.

Many of the inmates of the monastery fled to the Irish monastery at Bobbio in the Apennines to escape the massacre, taking with them the service books and other treasures. The monastery at Bobbio was founded in 598 by St Columbanus who had been educated in Bangor by St Comgall, its founder. St Columbanus left Ireland for the Continent and, after staying in Gaul for some time, he eventually crossed the Alps near Genoa in Italy,

Benedictus dominus deus from the Antiphonary of Bangor, 7th century

Audite omne ramantis
dm scam en eta
uiriinxpo beati
patrici episcupi
mo quodobonuobactu

where the Lombardic King Agilulf enabled him to build the monastery and where in 615 he died in seclusion.

It is thought that the Antiphonary of Bangor was taken by a famous Irishman named Dungal the Divine in 811 to the monastery at St Denis in Gaul where he became a recluse. He later retired to the monastery in Bobbio where he died, having bequeathed his library. In 1606 the library at Bobbio was transferred to the Ambrosian library in Milan.

The Antiphonary of Bangor is a thin manuscript volume consisting of 72 pages, roughly 230 × 180 mm (9" × 7") in size. The script is early Irish half-uncial, with an intermixture of minuscule, and was probably written by two scribes. There is very little ornament used in the manuscript and what there is is made up of clusters of three points in red surrounding certain initials; the calligraphy is in black.

Text beginning Audite omnes amantes from the Antiphonary of Bangor, 7th century

The Book of Durrow
MS A.4.5 (57) Trinity College Library, Dublin

Written around 680, the Book of Durrow is the earliest of the surviving fully illuminated Insular Gospel Books. It is 245 × 145 mm (9⅝" × 5⅝") in size, it contains canon-tables, carpet pages, full-page pictures of the Evangelist symbols, and the four types of ornamentation: Celtic motifs, ribbon interlace, animal interlace and rectilinear patterns such as check, diagonal fretwork, step and key patterns.

The place of manufacture is thought to have been a Columban monastery, but there is an argument over whether it was produced in Ireland, Northumbria or Iona. There is a colophon at the end of the book asking for prayers for the scribe St Columba so perhaps it is a copy of an earlier exemplar that may have been written by the saint. The Evangelist symbols opposite are very similar in style to animals found on earlier Pictish stone carvings.

Aldhelm of Malmesbury wrote in 686 to congratulate Eafrith on his six-year stay with the Irish, and it has been suggested that Eafrith and Eadfrith, who was thought to be the artist of the Lindisfarne Gospels around 698, are the same person, perhaps explaining why the Lindisfarne Gospels embody the tradition of Durrow. From its fusion of Celtic, Germanic and Mediterranean elements, the Book of Durrow is a treasure of illumination and imagination.

Detail from a carpet page, Book of Durrow, 7th century

Four Evangelist symbols, Book of Durrow, 7th century

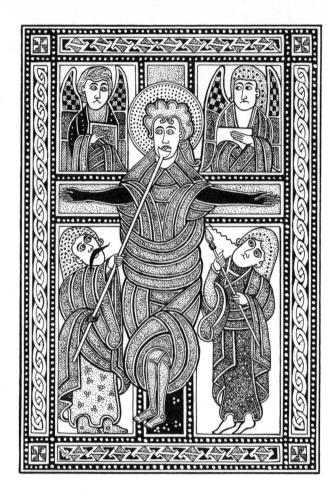

Eighth-Century Manuscripts

Celtic art of the 8th century is looked upon as being the beginning of a Golden Age because of its skilled craftsmanship and the precision of the detail in works such as the Tara brooch, with its chipped carved ornament and fine filigree and granular work, decorated with enamelled silver plates and glass beads. The Ardagh chalice, like the Tara brooch, was found in a hoard deposited away from Viking raiders and is one of the finest pieces of metalwork to survive from this period. Though there had been some earlier attacks in the 7th century, the raid that took place on Lambay Island off the coast of Dublin in 795 was the beginning of a series of sporadic assaults on all sides of the country. The fierce and sudden raids on the virtually defenceless monasteries brought terror to the monks and many were driven into exile by fear.

Crucifixion, St Gall Codex 51, 8th century

The Book of Mulling
MS A.I.15 (60)
Trinity College Library, Dublin

Besides the splendid Gospel Books, written and decorated in a grand manner for display on the altar, smaller 'pocket' Gospel Books were also produced – the Book of Mulling is a typical example, with the usual style of portraits. The books were light to carry, very practical and very economical, helping to explain why this style continued in production right into the 12th century, some four hundred years later. They were carried by the Irish monks in satchels and may have served the same function as the small Bibles or portable altar books carried by friars in later centuries.

The Book of Mulling was an immediate predecessor to the Book of Armagh. It came from the monastery at Tech-Molling (now St Mullins, County Carlow), which was founded by Saint Molingg who died in 698. The book was written in Irish minuscule and the colours used in the decoration and portraits include white, blue, green, yellow, ochre, brown, mauve, purple and cherry red. Produced in the mid-8th century, a subscription in a colophon at the end of St John's Gospel tells us that a scribe called Mulling executed the work.

Portrait of St John, Book of Mulling, 8th century

The size of the pages is 165 × 120 mm (6½" × 4¾").

There are now only three portraits of the Evangelists, each with borders of knotwork and interlaced animals with no symbols. One portrait is missing – originally they would have been seen at the beginning of each of the Gospels, but today they are assembled together at the end of the book. In a style reminiscent of the later Book of Kells, the portrait of St John shows him standing straight with a fixed forward gaze, legs wide apart, holding a large square book with both hands. His simple halo cuts into the outer frame (not shown) and gives the impression of the figure of the saint being pushed forward. The portraits are very similar in style to the Stowe Missal and the Gospel of St John in the Royal Irish Academy in Dublin. The stylized folds of the drapery and especially the tube-like folds can also be seen in the portraits in the St Gall Gospel Book.

There were eleven fragments from another Gospel found within the shrine that held the Book of Mulling, which include parts of the Gospels of St Matthew and St Mark. They were probably produced in the same scriptorium at Tech-Molling, although at a slightly later date.

Detail from the border on a portrait of St John, Book of Mulling, 8th century

Book of Dimma
MS A.4.23 (59) Trinity College Library, Dublin

The pocket Gospel Book of Dimma, which was 175 × 142 mm (6¾" × 5½") in size, was executed at the monastery at Roscrea, County Tipperary, in the second half of the 8th century. It has what is believed to be a false inscription attributing the work to a scribe named Dimma mac nathi who was a contemporary of Roscrea's founder, St Cronan, who died in 619. This inscription was probably made for political ends as the illumination and

Symbol of St John, Book of Dimma, 8th century

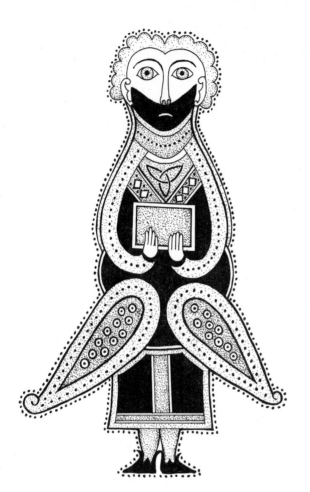

script were done by several hands. The Book of Dimma is particularly appealing for its rich colours of yellow, pink, orange, green and blue, and its style which can be compared to the St Gall Gospel Book.

Belonging to the Durrow tradition, the St John symbol on the previous page is seen as a frontal spreading eagle with an extra set of wings; its head is haloed and one of its talons is shown holding a book. St Mark is seen frontally and stern with a book held in front of him. Each of the Evangelists' portraits shows considerable stylization in the way drapery folds become independent forms ornamented with pattern. This form is similar to the earlier St Matthew symbol in the Echternach Gospels which was produced at Lindisfarne Library. There was considerable contact with other monastic centres in Ireland, Britain and Europe, and with Anglo-Saxon and Celtic styles of illumination at the time and many ideas were copied and adapted by the monks. A metal *Cumdach* made for the manuscript in the mid-12th century still survives.

Detail from the portrait of St Matthew, Book of Dimma, 8th century

Additional MS 40618
British Museum, London

Additional MS 40618 is a small manuscript measuring 127 × 102 mm (5" × 4") and contains sixty-six folios – an incomplete copy of the four Gospels. The only surviving illuminated picture is of St Luke, standing frontally holding a book, greatly resembling the portrait of the same saint in the Book of Mulling. The manuscript belongs to the group of Irish pocket Gospels of the second half of the 8th century, and was brought to England in the 10th or 11th centuries with its decoration unfinished. It was completed by the scribe Eduardus in the Winchester style.

Portrait of St Luke, Additional MS 40618, 8th century

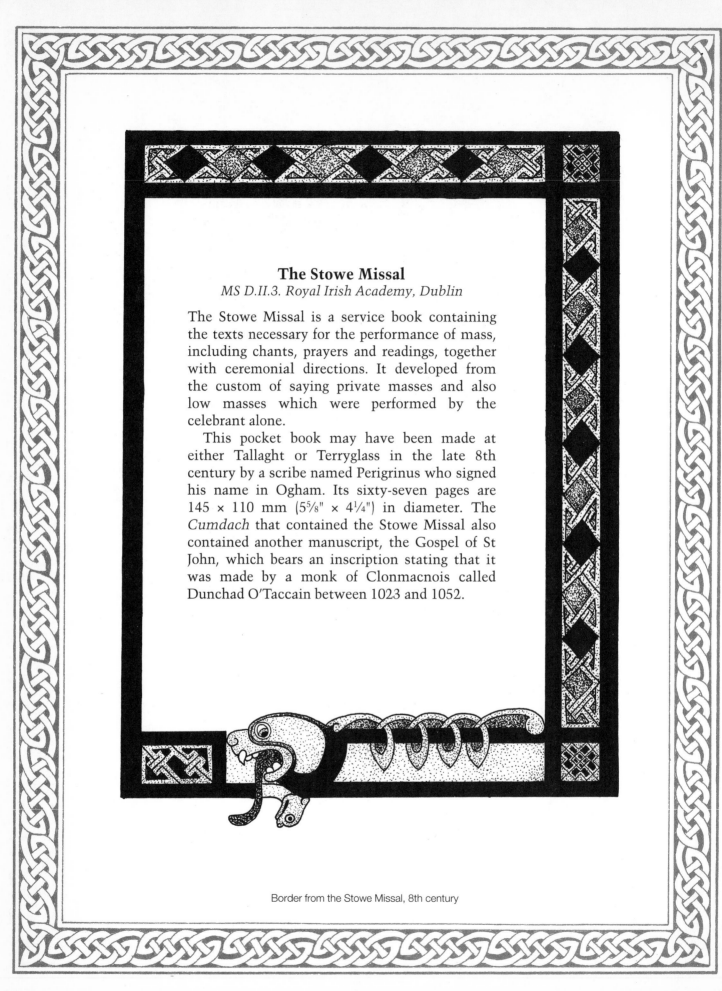

The Stowe Missal
MS D.II.3. Royal Irish Academy, Dublin

The Stowe Missal is a service book containing the texts necessary for the performance of mass, including chants, prayers and readings, together with ceremonial directions. It developed from the custom of saying private masses and also low masses which were performed by the celebrant alone.

This pocket book may have been made at either Tallaght or Terryglass in the late 8th century by a scribe named Perigrinus who signed his name in Ogham. Its sixty-seven pages are 145 × 110 mm (5⅝" × 4¼") in diameter. The *Cumdach* that contained the Stowe Missal also contained another manuscript, the Gospel of St John, which bears an inscription stating that it was made by a monk of Clonmacnois called Dunchad O'Taccain between 1023 and 1052.

Border from the Stowe Missal, 8th century

40

Gospel of St John
MS D.II.3. Royal Irish Academy, Dublin

An inscription in Ogham tells us that the Gospel of St John was executed by Perigrinus and perhaps at the same centre as the Stowe Missal, with which it is now bound, in the late 8th century. It has eleven pages which contain excerpts from the Gospel of St John.

Above the portrait of St John, the symbol of the eagle with its wings outstretched frames his head. The squat figure clasping his book is similar to the depiction of St John in the St Gall Gospel Book. Either side are panels of knotwork designs and key patterns.

Portrait of St John, Gospel of St John, 8th century

41

The Gospel Book of Cadmug
Bonifatianus 3. Landesbibliothek, Fulda

This mid-8th century manuscript belongs to the group of manuscripts of Irish pocket Gospel Books written by the scribe Cadmug. Its restitution was by tradition said to have been written by St Boniface who died in 754.

The Evangelist portraits are almost identical apart from their surrounding borders – they are represented frontally with a book in their left hands and a small sceptre in the right, and the colours are red, red-brown, violet, green and yellow. It was either produced in Ireland or by Irish hands on the Continent. Its style is rather weak and can be compared with the Book of Mulling.

St Luke, Gospel Book of Cadmug, mid-8th century

St Gall Gospel Book
Codex 51, Stiftsbibliothek, St Gall

The mid-8th century St Gall Gospel Book was probably written in Ireland and taken to the monastery at St Gall in Switzerland by an Irish monk in the 9th century. The Gospel has 268 pages and measures 295 × 215–220 mm (11½" × 8⅝"). The illumination consists of Evangelist portraits with facing initial pages. It has a fully illuminated Chi-Rho and carpet page, and is distinguished by having a last judgment page (*see* colour plate IV) and a crucifixion page. Its rich decoration is abstract and the colours, pink, brownish pink, mauve, yellow and blue are unusually bright. The decoration consists of simple interlace, key patterns, spirals and entwined animals.

St Matthew, St Gall Gospel Book, 8th century

Gospel of St John
Codex 60. Stiftsbibliothek, St Gall

The portrait of St John is similar in style to St Matthew in the Book of Dimma and the eagle above his head is similar to the portrait of St John in the St Gall Gospel Book – it is coloured in orange-yellow and black. The Gospel consists of sixty-eight pages which measure 268 × 190 mm (10½" × 7½"). Little is known of its origin, though it was probably made in Ireland.

Portrait of St John, Gospel of St John, 8th century

44

Codex 1395
Fragments 418–419, 422–423, 426–427, Stiftsbibliothek, St Gall

Codex 1395 consists of a series of single-leaf fragments that were bound together by the abbey librarian at St Gall in 1822.

St Matthew, Gospel Book fragment, 418– 419, Codex 1395, 8th century

Leaf 422–423 is a cross page on one page with prayers written at a later date on the other, this page may have been part of 418–419 at some time. The centre of the cross page is left blank and human figures decorate two of the panels of the cross, similar to those in the Macregol Gospel Book. The two other panels are filled with entwined birds.

Leaf 426–427 is an initial P with continuation capitals of a prayer on one side and the script continuing the prayer on the other. The decoration is similar to the St Gall Gospel Book and the Irish pocket Gospel Books. There is no reference to tell us when these documents reached the library at St Gall.

Leaf 418–419 contains the portrait of St Matthew on one side and charms against illness written by two scribes in the 9th century in Old Irish and Latin on the reverse. The bearded Evangelist, St Matthew, is seated with his legs to the right, though the upper portion of his body is facing forward, and his shoes are very similar to those of St Matthew in the Book of Dimma – they have free-standing tongues at the openings. He rests a knife on his book which has no support. A winged man, the symbol of St Matthew, is placed beside him.

Top: detail from an unidentified fragment, 426–427, Codex 1395, 8th century
Bottom: detail from a single-leaf cross page fragment, 422–423, Codex 1395, 8th century

Gospel Book Garland of Howth
Codex Usserianus Secundas
MS A.4.6 (56) Trinity College Library, Dublin

The illuminated pages of the Gospel Book consist of two initial pages for Saints Matthew and Mark and are both badly damaged – only the orange minimum survives. There is a little white and yellow, but the traces of blue are almost gone.

On the Initial page St Mark stands between the stems of the 'IN' monogram, and his symbol, the lion, is above him. The tubular folds in his garment are similar to the portraits in the earlier Irish pocket Gospels. The book was found near Howth on the island 'Ireland's Eye' and was believed to have been owned by the historian Archbishop James Ussher.

Initial from the Gospel Book Garland of Howth, 8th century

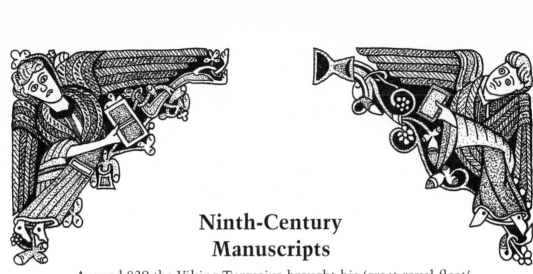

Ninth-Century
Manuscripts

Around 830 the Viking Turgesius brought his 'great royal fleet' of fair-haired Norsemen, the *Finn-ghaill*, to the north of Ireland and began to found colonies, establishing a stronghold by the Dubh/Linn (black pool) at the ford of the Liffey. Other fleets followed and began to settle. One by one the great monasteries were plundered and burned and the abbots and monks murdered. Turgesius assumed the abbacy at Armagh for himself but was finally captured by the King of Meath and was drowned in Lough Owel.

Shortly after the death of Turgesius, the Vikings came under attack from the *Dubh-ghaill*, a band of Danish marauders along the east coast, and the Vikings began to kill each other. The attacks were fiercely resisted, the Danes finally defeated and Dublin had a new Norse leader, Olaf the White.

Aed Finnliaith, the Irish High King, began courageously attacking and destroying Norse strongholds in the North, his army carrying the *Bachall Ísa*, an enshrined relic of the True Cross, with them into battle. They cleared the Vikings from the north of Dublin and never returned. The Vikings now fell upon middle and southern Ireland, and a Munster chronicler tells how they ravaged the churches and sanctuaries, destroying and stealing the reliquaries and books. After 880, with the outbreak of a dynastic struggle at home and the constant pressure from the Irish, the number of raids began to diminish and there was an uneasy lull in Viking attacks.

The Irish monks who left earlier took with them many of the sacred books for safe keeping and they are now in various libraries in Europe. A new Irish movement of missionaries began the journey to the Carolingian Empire and the court of Charlemagne, who welcomed them for their faith, but also for their learning of the Irish schools.

Angels from the Book of Kells, 9th century

The writings of Dicuil, an Irishman at the Carolingian Court, included tracts on grammar, astronomy and geography, but it was in the second half of the century in Liège that the Irish scholar Sedilius Scottus and his companions reached their greatest renown – their standard of learning was the highest in Europe.

By the end of the century very little manuscript illumination was being undertaken in Ireland and the quality of its metalworking became inferior to the earlier period. Filigree and chip carving were no longer done and the delicacy and minuteness of detail disappeared due to the Viking raiders.

Symbol of St Matthew, Book of Kells, 9th century

Book of Armagh

MS 52, Trinity College Library,
Dublin

The colophons in the Book of Armagh show it to be the work of Ferdomnagh, a scribe at Armagh, who died, according to the Annals of Ulster, in 845. The colophons also tell us that he worked under the direction of Torbach, who was the abbot of Armagh for only one year (807–8).

The volume in fine minuscule script contains three distinct parts. The first documents are in Latin and Irish and relate to the life of St Patrick and the rights of his church in Armagh to primacy over other Irish monasteries and its right to levy St Patrick's tribute. It also includes the Confession of St Patrick, the biographical notes compiled in the 7th century by Muirchú an Tirechán, and a few other Patrician documents. The second section

Initial and text from the Book of Armagh, 9th century

contains the only complete New Testament text which has survived from Early Christian Ireland and finally Sulpicius Severus' Life of St Martin (who it is thought was an uncle to Patrick). The fine-quality initials with animal heads, birds, fish, interlace and trumpet spirals are decorated with black-and-white line drawings.

The Evangelist symbols can be compared to those in the Book of Kells – they all have four wings, but none have haloes and only the men hold a book. St Luke holds a bust of the other three symbols on their wings to emphasize the concordance of the Gospels. The book size is 195 × 145 mm (7⅝" × 5⅝") and fits into the category of pocket Gospel Books.

In 937 a *Cumdach*, which has not survived, was provided for the manuscript by Donnchadh, son of Flan, King of Ireland. However, an 11th-century leather book satchel stamped with interlace and zoomorphic patterns does still exist.

Symbol of St Luke, Book of Armagh, 9th century

Book of Kells

MS A.1.6 (58) Trinity College Library, Dublin

Described in 1007 in the Annals of Ulster as 'The great Gospel of Columkille, the chief relic of the Western World', the Book of Kells is the most famous of all the Insular manuscripts and is at the pinnacle of Celtic draughtsmanship and would never be equalled again. The full-page decorations are separate from the main body of text – this was possibly so that the work could be undertaken by several hands on separate sheets of vellum with apprentices filling in the details. This way there would have been control over which pages were of the high standard to be included in the finished bound book.

It was originally thought to have had 350 pages of which only 340 remain, and was possibly begun on Iona, but because of the constant raids by the Vikings it was transferred with the relics of St Columba to the new monastery at Kells for completion in 807. Both Iona and Kells were governed as a single community. Like the Book of Durrow, they share the same arrangement of Gospels and a number of Pictish-style ornaments.

The Annals of Ulster tell us that the book was stolen from the great stone church of Cenannas but 'was found after twenty nights and two months with its gold stolen from it, buried in the ground.' The book is 330 × 250 mm (13" × 9¾") in size after being trimmed by a 19th-century binder and is now bound in four volumes.

Portrait of Christ, Book of Kells, 9th century

Detail from Breves causae of St Matthew, Book of Kells, 9th century

Macdurnan Gospels
MS 1370, Lambeth Palace, London

The Gospel Book was named after Máel Brigte Mac Durnan, the abbot of Armagh (888–927), who was also head of all the Columban monasteries. The script is similar to the earlier Book of Armagh which was written by Ferdomnagh at Armagh, though the style of decoration differs as it is orderly and well planned – it could have been entrusted to another artist to execute. The colours are mostly purple, green and orange with white used on the face, hands and feet of the Evangelists. The paint is very thick and has an enamel-like finish.

Each of the Gospels starts with a portrait and a large initial page which are similar to those in the Book of Armagh and may have been inspired by it. In size it is slightly smaller than the Book of Armagh – 158 × 111 mm (6¼" × 4¼"). The Macdurnan Gospels belong to a group of Irish pocket Gospel Books. The manuscripts' illumination which is still in perfect condition was given to Christ Church, Canterbury, by King Athelstan (d. 939).

XPI from the Macdurnan Gospels, 9th century

St Matthew from the Macdurnan Gospels, 9th century

Macregol/Rushworth Gospels
MS Auct. D.2.19 (S.C. 3946)
Bodleian Library, Oxford

A colophon written on the last page within a frame of interlace states that the scribe and painter of this gospel was Mac Regol (d. 820), who was abbot of Birr (Offaly) which was founded by St Brendan (d. 571). In the Annals of the Four Masters, a list of deaths of ecclesiastics, Mac Regol's title of scribe appears before any other title as it was considered a great honour to write out the words of the Gospels. The Annals list the names of many scribes but through the ravages of the Vikings and over time their work has disappeared and we can only wonder at what has been lost. Though there is no trace of the monastery today, the old well of St Brendan still bubbles out of a shelf of rock and into the river Camcor.

It has an Evangelist page and an initial page at the start of each Gospel. The thickly applied colours are still bright and are in golden yellow, bright red, violet, green, black and a shade of brown. This remarkable scribe does not seem to have had any use for a compass in his drawing which is irregular and at some points reckless in its improvisation, and though the script is large, it is simple and majestic.

This de luxe Gospel Book consists of 169 leaves of thick and coarse vellum measuring 348 × 264 mm (13⅝" × 10⅜") in size and is one of the largest of the Irish Gospel Books. The portrait of St Matthew has been lost as the book has passed through history – it bears traces of having been roughly handled and exposed to all weather conditions.

Border design from the Macregol Gospels, 9th century

Detail from the beginning of St Matthew's Gospel, Macregol Gospels, 9th century

Priscian, Periegesis Dionysii and Institutiones Grammaticae
B.P.L. 67 Universiteitsbibliotheek, Leiden

Priscianus Caesariensis was a 6th-century Italian Latin grammarian who taught in Constantinople and wrote many texts including the *Institutiones Grammaticae* which had a profound influence on the teaching of Latin in Europe.

There are similarities in the line initials that make it likely that they were done by the scribes who worked on the Book of Armagh. A colophon in the book says that it was copied by a scribe named Dubtach in 838, and was taken to Soissons in the 9th century. It contains 207 pages and is 225 × 160 mm (8¾" × 6¼") in size.

Initial from B.P.L. 67, 9th century

Turin Gospels
*Codex O.IV.20 Biblioteca
Nazionale, Turin*

There are four pages left of this Gospel Book and it is now no more than a wreck, but the four illuminated pages that do remain are decorated to a high standard that can be compared in elaborateness to the Book of Kells.

Originally 280 × 196 mm (11" × 7¾") in size, the book is slightly smaller than Kells. The layout and some of the profile faces of the interlace figures are similar in style to the St Gall, Macregol and Macdurnan Gospels and could have been the product of the same scriptorium some fifty years later.

The Turin Gospels have gone through a series of tragedies since they reached Bobbio in the 9th century – at one stage it was used as a source of vellum and its text erased. In 1904 a fire at the Turin Library destroyed 185 of the pages, the four that remain were displayed separately and were saved although they are in a poor condition, badly shrunk and the colour of old leather. These four pages contain two carpet pages and two full-page miniatures, one of the Ascension, the other of the Last Judgment.

Detail from the Last Judgment, Turin Gospels, 9th century

Priscian Institutiones Grammaticae
MS Cod. 904 Stiftsbibliothek, St Gall

This manuscript was written at Armagh around 850 and is important because of its large number of Irish glosses which include personal comments by the scribes attributed to the book – Maelpatric, Finguinne and Donngus. Like the MS B.P.L. 67 it has similarities to the Book of Armagh. It was taken to Cologne between 850 and 869 and from there found its way to St Gall. The book is 398 × 280 mm (15⅝" × 11") in size and has 120 pages.

Initial from Priscian Institutiones Grammaticae, 9th century

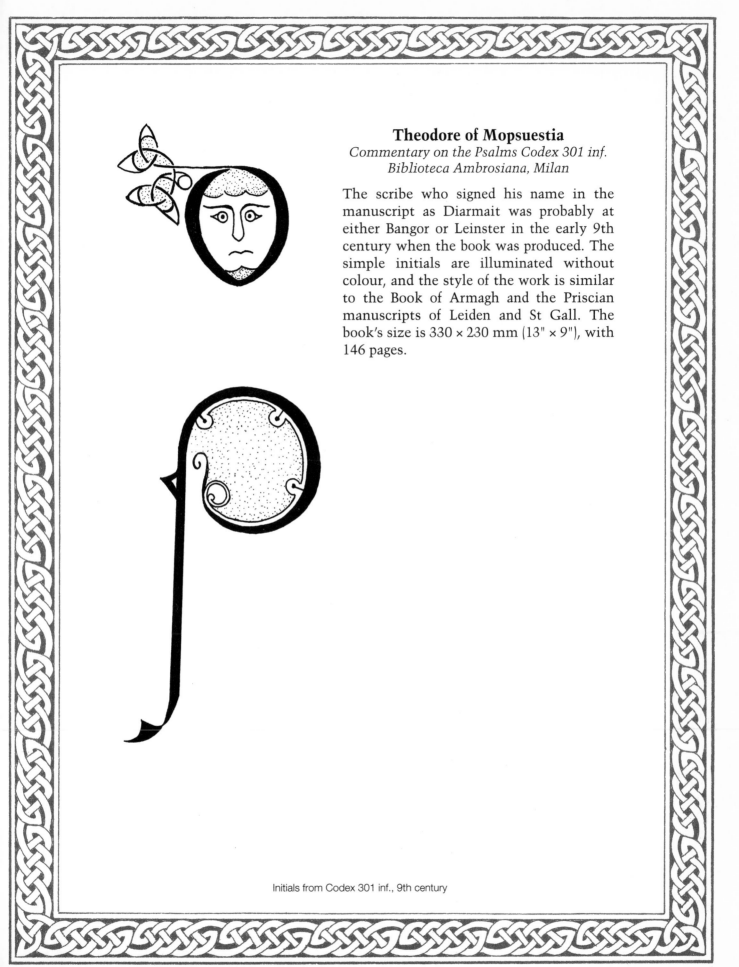

Theodore of Mopsuestia
Commentary on the Psalms Codex 301 inf.
Biblioteca Ambrosiana, Milan

The scribe who signed his name in the manuscript as Diarmait was probably at either Bangor or Leinster in the early 9th century when the book was produced. The simple initials are illuminated without colour, and the style of the work is similar to the Book of Armagh and the Priscian manuscripts of Leiden and St Gall. The book's size is 330 × 230 mm (13" × 9"), with 146 pages.

Initials from Codex 301 inf., 9th century

Tenth-Century Manuscripts

Even though the High King Niall Glúndubh was killed and his strong force of Irish chiefs was defeated in 919 at Islandbridge by the Vikings, still the Norsemen were unable to subdue Ireland to their rule. From the hills of eastern County Clare, two brothers Mathghamhain and Brian Boru began a long guerrilla war against the Norsemen at Limerick until 967 when the King of Limerick brought his full power against them in a decisive battle at Sulchóid and lost and the city was sacked. Brian Boru became King of Munster after his brother had been murdered and eventually in 1002 became powerful enough to take the High Kingship itself. A manuscript called *The War* tells us that Brian Boru sent learned scholars out of Ireland to bring back books to replace those destroyed by the Norse plunderers.

The only manuscripts that have survived from the 10th and 11th centuries are all psalters and copies of St Jerome's second revision of the Latin text of psalms known as the Gallican version. In each of the manuscripts the 150 psalms are divided into three groups of fifty (na trí cóicait) – these were recited by the Irish monks at three different offices every day. These divisions are not found in the only pre-10th-century psalter that has survived – the Cathach. The beginning of each section is marked by a figured page on the verso (the left-hand page) and a framed page with a large initial on the recto (the right-hand page). On the Continent the psalters have a variety of arrangements and divisions.

Running hare from the Double Psalter of St Ouen, 10th century

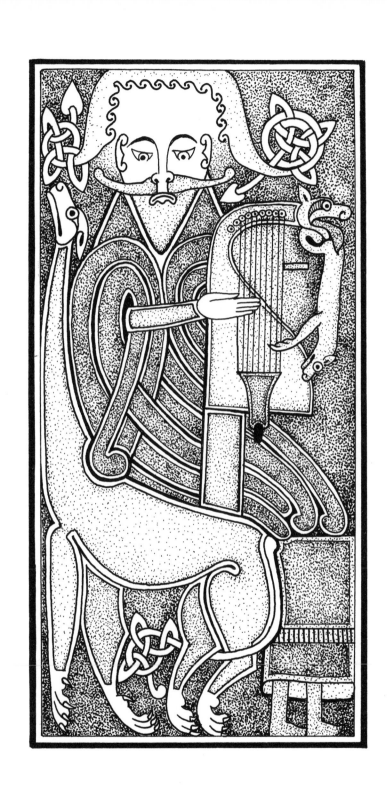

Adaptation of David playing the harp, Cotton MS Vitellius F.XI, 10th century

Cotton MS Vitellius F.XI
British Library, London

This manuscript was badly damaged in a fire at Ashburnham House, London, along with the whole cotton collection in 1731. Its pages are shrunken and discoloured and the beginning and end of the book are now lost – only fifty-nine pages remain and they contain 137 psalms. The pages are 165 × 120 mm (6½" × 4¾") in size.

The two remaining fully decorated pages of David the Musician and David and Goliath are now bound at the beginning of the manuscript. The colours, although now altered or faded, were deep purple, an orange-red, yellow and pink.

An Irish colophon in the book suggests that it may have been produced at the monastery at Monasterboice. The colophon was lost in the fire, but was copied by Archbishop Ussher: 'The blessing of God on Muiredach ... the scholar.' The pages show a great similarity in their style and realism to the images carved on the early 10th-century Cross of Muiredach at Monasterboice and the stone cross of Scriptures at Clonmacnois suggesting a close inter-relation between the two arts.

Initials from Cotton MS Vitellius F.XI, 10th century

The Double Psalter of St Ouen
MS 24 (A.41) Bibliothèque Municipale, Rouen

In the 11th or 12th centuries the Double Psalter of St Ouen reached a Benedictine monastery in Normandy from Ireland, possibly brought by an Irish traveller on his way to Rome, and from there it was taken to the Benedictine monastery of St Ouen in Rouen.

The Psalter has 310 pages in all, four of which are written by another hand and at a later date and contain prayers and canticles. The book is 240 × 165 mm (9⅜" × 6½"), which is larger than the Cotton MS Vitellius F.XI, but slightly smaller than the Southampton Psalter. The script has much in common with both of them. There are 300 capitals which are all of a knotted wire type and finely drawn and originate from initials in the Book of Kells and are also found in the later Priscian and Macdurnan manuscripts. Those initials that begin the psalms are still simple and have a little colour.

It is believed that the Psalter was probably used as a study book rather than a choir book because it has a great number of abbreviations but no collects or canticles at the end of each section. There is a similarity in one of the rough doodle drawings on a border of a little man with outstretched fingers to that found in Byzantine manuscripts when an important passage needed to be stressed.

Initials from the Double Psalter of St Ouen, 10th century

Eleventh-Century Manuscripts

Brian Boru visited the ecclesiastical capital of Ireland in 1004 and had his scribe enter his name in the Book of Armagh as Brian, Imperator Scottorum. Ten years later at the battle of Clontarf, Brian, as High King of Ireland, would face the last great rally of the Vikings and their allies outside the walls of Dublin. In a battle that is celebrated in Scandinavian and Irish literature he lost his life, but the power of the Vikings in Ireland was broken.

A cultural revival in metalwork began at the end of the 10th century, though the quality of the workmanship never matched the earlier Armagh chalice and Tara brooch, and gradually in the early 11th century they began to regain something of their old skills. The three small shrines of Soiscél Molaise, Stowe Missal and Breac Maodhóg draw from the old Irish skills, though not on their level of intricacy – the new work shows the development of the beginnings of a true Romanesque art. Their style of work was also influenced by the Scandinavian patterns Ringerike, Urnes and Jellinge – Scandinavian techniques in metalwork and silver and niello inlaying also appear in some Irish carvings.

The church was still well organized, as it had been in the 7th century by the monasteries – walled villages with huts and small churches were still apparent. The 11th century saw the beginning of an ecclesiastical change in the Irish church, and priests began to be sent by Dublin to Canterbury to be consecrated as bishops. Eventually the archbishops of Canterbury claimed jurisdiction over the Irish church and urged reforms within church affairs. In spite of the exodus of many of its scribes to Europe because of the destructive power of the Vikings, the art of Irish illumination continued, but in a weaker form.

Initial from the Southampton Psalter, 11th century

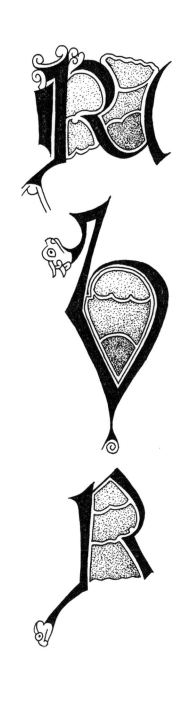

The Book of Dun Cow

*MS 23.E.25 Royal Irish
Academy, Dublin*

Situated in the centre of Ireland, the monastery of Clonmacnois in which the Book of Dun Cow (also known as the Lebor na Huidre) was produced was a centre of study and artistic endeavour and was rich and influential.

The Annals of the Four Masters are partly attributed to the abbot of Clonmacnois, Tigernach Ua Broein, who tells us that the scribe Máel Muire Mac Célechair was killed by brigands in the Cathedral of Clonmacnois in 1106. His family worked on the Dun Cow and possibly the first section of MS Rawlinson B502 – their skills as scribes and illuminators had been handed down from generation to generation, from Ferdomnagh the scribe of the Book of Armagh.

The Book of Dun Cow is a miscellaneous collection of verse and prose and was in the keeping of St Ciaran, the founder of Clonmacnois, on his journey to study in Clonard.

The skin from a pet cow of St Ciaran, which was wrapped around the book and from where the book got its name, was highly revered and it was believed that to lie on it when close to death would ensure the soul a happy journey to the other world. The book is now badly mutilated and discoloured with only 67 pages remaining, measuring 280 × 200 mm (11" × 7⅞"). It is written in thick black ink on badly prepared and patched vellum sheets and except for slightly more elaborate initials, the delicate initials chiefly belong to both a wire and ribbon style of decoration with small animal heads as terminals. The small amount of colour – yellow, purple and red lead – is very faded.

Initials from the Book of Dun Cow, 11th century

MS Rawlinson B502
Bodleian Library, Oxford

Much care was taken by the monasteries, which from the 11th century began to flourish again, as they started to study and collect early Irish text from what was left after the ravages of the Vikings and a series of books such as the Book of Dun Cow and the slightly later Rawlinson B502 were produced to preserve the writings of, for instance, epics, poems, genealogies.

The first section of the Rawlinson B502 consists of a fragment of the 'Annals of Tigernach' named after Tigernach Ua Broein, the abbot of the monastery at Clonmacnois who died in 1088. In the second section the pages are dark and the colours faded. It contains the Saltair na Rann – the psalter of the Quatrains which is a long biblical poem in Irish. Other poems and genealogies point to a monastery at Leinster as the possible place of its origin. Although thought to be of a later date, it shows the same style of decoration as the Liber Hymnorum. It is badly trimmed to keep it the size of the first section and now measures 295 × 220 mm (11½" × 8⅝") and only seventy pages remain.

Decoration from MS Rawlinson B502, 11th century

68

Initial from MS Rawlinson B502, 11th century

Southampton Psalter
MS C.9 (59) St John's College, Cambridge

This a complete psalter of ninety-eight pages, which measure 270 × 175 mm (10½" × 6¾"), that continues the tradition of earlier psalters in its division into three sections, 'Fifties', of psalms and because of its glosses is dated between the late 10th and early 11th centuries. It contains many elements of the earlier Cotton MS Vitellius F.XI, especially in the figure page of David and Goliath, and although some details have been omitted in the later book, such as David's sling, it is obvious that the artist must have seen and been inspired by it. Overall the figure pictures in the Southampton Psalter do not have the same strength as the Cotton F.XI, though it makes up for it in its use of colourful patchwork infilling on the figures.

It has a decorated initial at the start of each psalm, which is coloured with yellow, orange and mauve, and the other initials are of the ribbon and wire type and used alternately throughout the book in yellow, brownish purple, lighter purple and orange.

Initial from the Southampton Psalter, 11th century

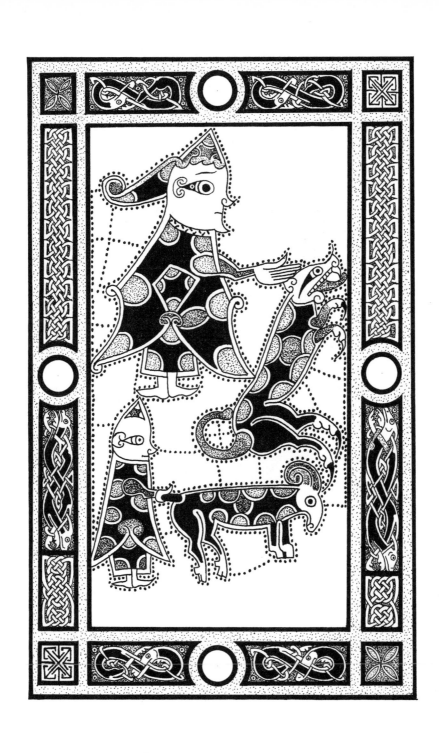

David fighting the lion, Southampton Psalter, 11th century

Psalter of St Caimin

MS A.1. Library of the Franciscan House of Celtic Studies and Historical Research, Killiney, County Dublin

The psalter of St Caimin is all that is left of the high-quality manuscripts that were produced at the ancient monastery of Inis Cealtra on the small island of Lough Derg, forty miles south of Clonmacnois. The psalter gets its name from the saint who lived in Inis Cealtra in the 7th century and who we are unreliably told in its second folio also wrote it. It had been attacked by the Vikings as well and in 922 they came again under Tomrar, son of Elge, and plundered the shores of Lough Derg – many of its relics and shrines were thrown into the water and lost. Brian Boru helped in the rebuilding of the monastery of which his brother Marcan was the abbot.

It is a large book, 340 × 255 mm (13¼" × 10") in size, carefully written in terms of its layout and execution – simple capitals are inserted within the text and there is an overall feeling of elegance in the work. The book is not a complete psalter and consists of two portions of Psalm 118 (*Beati immaculati*) in the Vulgate version; it is possible that the book originally had 200 pages. Because of the similarities to the Book of Dun Cow, it may have been produced at Clonmacnois by the same scribes.

Initials from the Psalter of St Caimin, 11th century

Epistle of St Paul

MS Lat. 1247
Nationalbibliothek, Vienna

Muiredach Mac Robartaig, a monk from the north of Ireland, was a member of the Donegal family entrusted with the safe keeping of the Cathach of St Columba. He stayed for a year in 1067 at the monastery at Bamberg in Germany where he was persuaded by an Irishman to settle there and to forget his proposed pilgrimage to Rome with his two companions. A small Irish community known as Weih-Sankt-Peter was formed in the town of Ratisbon.

From Weih-Sankt-Peter Muiredach, or Marianus Scottus of Mainz as he was known in Germany, began the 160 pages of the Epistle of St Paul on 23 March and it was completed by 17 May. Written in a Continental type of minuscule, it has glosses and a commentary with strong Irish features.

The initials are mainly large and simple, though they gradually sprout animal heads and simple interlace endings as the book progresses, recalling the type of decoration he would have known from the Irish scriptoriums.

Initial from the Epistle of St Paul, 11 century

Chronicle of Marianus Scottus
MS Lat. 830 Vatican Library, Rome

The Marianus Scottus Chronicle was copied in around 1072 at the monastery of St Martin at Mainz by an Irish scribe, Máel Brigte, who was born in 1028 and became a monk at Mag-bile (Molville, County Down). At the suggestion of his abbot, Tigernach Bairrcech, he sought exile from Ireland after some small occurrence. He went to various monasteries before reaching St Kilian at Würzburg where he was ordained and then at Fulda he became a walled-up recluse. In 1069 he moved to another walled-up cell at St Martin of Mainz where he completed the compilation of his manuscript. Another Irish exile, probably in an adjacent cell, copied the manuscript for him. He died in about 1082.

The book is made up of 170 pages, 250 × 290 mm (9¾" × 11⅜") in size. The foliage decoration on the initials has similarities to the Scandinavian Jellinge and Ringerike styles, and the chronicle relates the history of the world since the Creation.

Initial from the Chronicle of Marianus Scottus, 11th century

74

Drummond Missal

MS 627 Pierpont Morgan Library, New York

A small missal measuring 150 × 115 mm (5⅞" × 4½") in size, the text is written in Irish minuscule with majuscule in some parts on the 109 pages. The Drummond Missal came from the monastic centre at Glendalough, which was founded by St Kevin in the late 6th century, and contains a missal preceded by a calendar, which from the names mentioned dates the manuscript to around 1061. There is a poem in the form of a dialogue between St Kevin and St Ciaran of Sier, whom he welcomes to Leinster on the final page, and a number of Irish poems written in the margins. The decoration consists of fine calligraphic touches with the initials embellished with animal, spiral and vegetable terminals. There are similarities in style to the Book of Dun Cow, with yellow and red used as infill colours.

There is no information about how the missal reached Drummond Castle in Perthshire in the 18th century – it was mislaid for some time and then re-discovered in 1861 and left the castle in 1916.

Initials from the Drummond Missal, 11th century

Liber Hymnorum
*MS A.4.2. Trinity College
Library, Dublin*

The Liber Hymnorum in Trinity College Library is an earlier version than the one in the Franciscan Library at Killiney. The text is similar, but not identical and they are arranged in a different order. Both are in a poor state and have darkened badly.

The hymnal, 200 × 125 mm (7⅞" × 5") in size, is a collection of hymns in Latin and Irish and was probably meant for choir use as the features are large enough to be seen by a number of people at the same time. It contains thirty-four pages of which only twenty-eight belong to the original text – the rest are irregular gatherings of additional material.

Each hymn starts with a large ornamental initial beast either in the ribbon style or the dominantly straight line type. Most have foliage ornament mixed with the animal initial, a style that is thought to have fully developed by 1071, by which time the scribe of the Marianus Scottus Chronicle had left Ireland. He later incorporated it in his work. All are well drawn and elaborate, with green, red, yellow and purple used in the illumination. The first letter of each verse is also filled in with a bright colour. The system of overdotting from the St Gall Gospel Book three centuries earlier is again used, as well as the dots surrounding the larger initials. At one time the manuscript must have looked glorious.

Initial from the Liber Hymnorum, 11th century

Twelfth-Century Manuscripts

Muirchertach Ua Brian, King of Munster, with the help of Gilla Espuic, the Bishop of Limerick, an Irishman who held no allegiance to Canterbury, and the support of other Irish churchmen in 1110 achieved their first triumph in the reform of the Irish Church. At a national synod convened at Rath Bresail, near Cashel, Muirchertach and other laity and clergy drew up a new constitution providing two archbishops and twenty-four bishops with fixed sees and delimited dioceses, although it took another forty years for the reform to overcome the vested interests of the Irish monasteries.

Around 1119, Cellach of Armagh and St Malachy of Armagh began to reform the diocese of Armagh, 'rooting out barbarous rites' according to St Bernard. When Malachy became Bishop of Armagh he immediately began making plans for a new national synod, and the arrangements took him twice to Rome. On the first return journey he left some of his companions with St Bernard at Clairvaux to be trained as novices in the Cistercian order. In 1141 St Bernard wrote to Malachy calling on him to prepare a place in Ireland for a Cistercian monastery to be built. After returning from his second visit to the Pope he died at Clairvaux. The synod he planned was convened four years after his death.

The land for the site for the abbey church at Mellifont was given by the King of Airghialla, Donnchadh Ua Cerbhaill, and work began in 1142. With the help of some of St Bernard's monks and his architect, the Cistercian complex was completed and consecrated in 1157 and ushered in the building of a number of other sister abbeys of Mellifont in Ireland, marking the end of the old Irish monastic age.

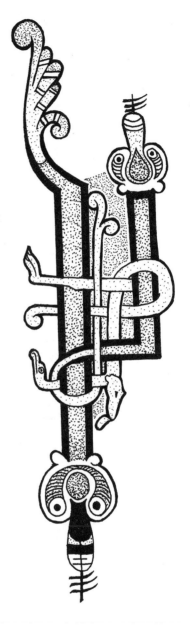

Initial from the Coupar Angus Psalter, 12th century

77

Liber Hymnorum

MS A.2. Library of Franciscan House of Celtic Studies, Dublin

The first mention of the Franciscan volume of the Liber Hymnorum states that it was housed in the Franciscan Friary in Donegal in 1630. At 205 × 115 mm (8" × 4½") it is similar in size to the earlier MS A.4.2 Liber Hymnorum in Trinity College Library, Dublin, but has only twenty-three pages and in spite of the similarities between the books, the Franciscan manuscript has weaker and smaller decoration, with less use of colour and is the work of different scribes, though possibly at the same scriptorium twenty to thirty years later. The initials alternate between the ribbon and wire styles with entwined foliage; the wire initials are similar to those in the 10th-century Double Psalter. Linguistic forms within the manuscript indicate that it is later than the Trinity College manuscript.

Initials from the Liber Hymnorum, 12th century

Book of Leinster

MS H.2.18 Trinity College
Library, Dublin
MS A.3. Franciscan House of Celtic
Studies, Dublin

The Book of Leinster at Trinity College Library has 177 pages and only ten pages in the Franciscan Library, and is on average 330 × 230 mm (13" × 9") in size. It is written in two or more columns in a rough Irish minuscule.

Entries in the book tell us that it was written in Terryglass, near Lough Derg, by the abbot, Aed Húa Crimthainn, who collected the material from many books, including the Ulster epic, Táin Bó Cúailnge. It is thought to have been started post 1152 and completed after a good deal of travelling, gathering the material around 1161, and it continued to be added to up until Aed's death in the 13th century.

The only initial of some note is the one at the beginning of the Táin Bó Cúailnge which includes a very bright pink in the colouration. The smaller capitals, which have beasts, snakes, foliage and animal and human heads, are added to the terminals.

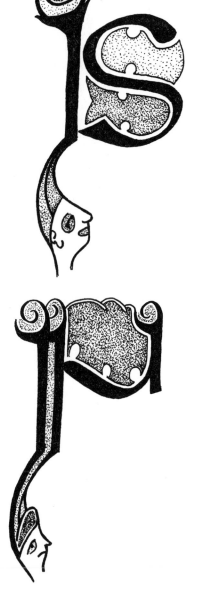

Initials from the Book of Leinster, 12th century

Corpus Missal

MS 282, Corpus Christi College
Library, Oxford

The decoration in the Corpus Missal is similar to the Scandinavian Urnes style of decoration – the entwined beasts are more elongated than earlier beast ornamentation and there are sinuous snakes' bodies whose heads are seen from above.

The missal is 170 × 120 mm (6¾" × 4¾") in size and contains 212 pages and though damaged, it still has part of its original binding of wooden boards, and the course vellum pages are dark and uneven. It is kept in a leather satchel which would have been too tight for it to have contained the manuscript when it was complete.

Though there is no history of the missal before it reached the college, similarities with the decoration on the panels of the Cross of Cong suggest that it may have been produced in the first quarter of the 12th century.

There is a story that it was found in an Irish bog though there is no evidence and this may be no more than a legend.

It is a Roman Missal and is generously decorated with elaborate capitals which appear on practically every page. They are all coloured in a striking colour scheme of bright blue, reddish purple – a rich yellow on a background of deep red. The location where it was written and the scribe are unknown.

Initial from the Corpus Missal, 12th century

80

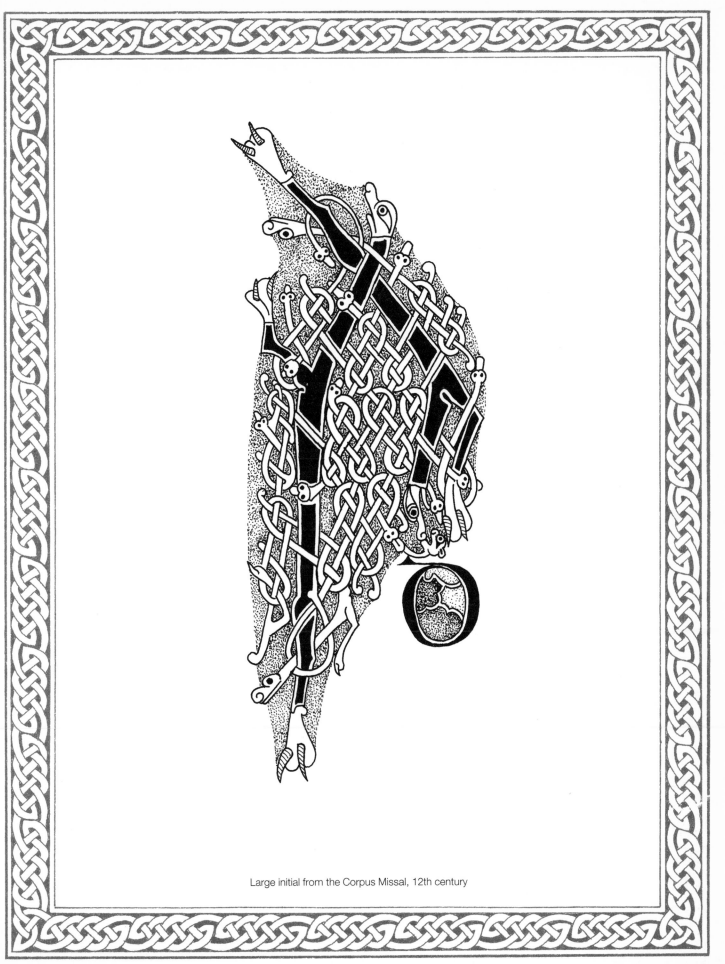

Large initial from the Corpus Missal, 12th century

De Consolatione of Boetius

MS LXXVII Biblioteca Medicea Laurenziana, Florence

This volume of forty-seven pages, 250 × 170 mm (9¾" × 6¾") in size, contains the 'De Consolatione Philosophiae' of Boetius, a Roman philosopher, orator, poet and statesman, who is thought to have lived from 480 until 524.

There are only a few decorative initials in this book though they show inventiveness and originality in their composition. Some are similar to the Corpus Missal, but they are less stylized. One of the initials of a twisted human figure with a pointed hat resembles a bronze figure on the shrine of St Manchan. The colours are red and yellow. The date for the manuscript is thought to be the same as the Corpus Missal – the first quarter of the 12th century.

Initials from De Consolatione of Boetius, 12th century

The Psalter of Cormac

Add. MS 36929, British Library, London

The quality of the decoration is high in this small psalter and it has a unique music colophon at the end of the canticles in the first 'Fifty'. The lines of music are on four staves in red and black and clearly belong to the 12th century.

The scribe signs his name: Cormacus scripsit on one of the 179 pages, which measure 170 × 130 mm (6¾" × 5"). It is mostly written in Irish majuscule with great care taken over its uniformity. The large initials vary – they are colourful, highly imaginative and are surrounded by a web of complicated knotwork with leaf, head and tail terminals. Each psalm also has smaller ribbon and wire types of entwined beast initials, similar in style to Liber Hymnorum and St Caimin manuscripts.

Large initial from the Psalter of Cormac, 12th century

Egerton MS 3323
British Museum, London

This manuscript consists of two leaves of vellum measuring 220 × 170 mm (8⅝" × 6¾"), with two different treatises written in Irish minuscule. The two initials are simple black letters and they are close to the decoration of the Drummond Missal.

One of the pages has a note written in Irish: 'We are here in Glendalough on the day of Pentecost. It is a pity that Tuathal is ailing', an additional note mentions that he died that night. Tuathal was the abbot of Glendalough and died in 1106.

Psalter (Galba)
MS Cotton Galba A.V.
British Library, London

Badly damaged in the Cotton Library fire at Ashburnham House in London in 1731, the thirty-five pages which measure 120 × 90 mm (4¾" × 3½") have been shrunken by the heat, turned dark brown and split. The manuscript is a psalter with a tripartite division with canticles and collects at the end like many of the Irish psalters and has large initials at the beginning of each 'Fifty', and small ribbon and wire initials at the beginning of each psalm. The style and artistry of this psalter is very poor; the colour is a deep reddish purple – red lead and yellow.

Top: initial from Egerton MS 3323, 12th century
Bottom: initial from Psalter (Galba), 12th century

Rosslyn Missal

MS 18.5.19, National Library of Scotland, Edinburgh

The text in this book, like the Drummond Missal and the Corpus Missal, is the same as a Roman Missal. The simple ribbon designs of beasts and snakes in the illumination are similar in style and though the colours are faded, they are delicate and lightly applied to the vellum. The overall feeling of the missal is of elegance and simplicity. The book is 170 × 120 mm (6¾" × 4¾") in size and contains 135 pages.

It is thought to have been written for the re-dedication of the cathedral at Downpatrick after the death of St Malachy who was bishop there from 1137 to 1148. Formerly consecrated to the Holy Trinity, it was now claimed as the burial place of St Patrick and re-dedicated to him. By 1183 the bodies of Saints Brigit and Columba were also claimed to have been found and enshrined in the cathedral.

Initials from the Rosslyn Missal, 12th century

Coupar Angus Psalter
Palatine MS Lat.65. Vatican Library, Rome

The Coupar Angus Psalter is a large psalter measuring 220 × 310 mm (8⅝" × 12¼") and contains 197 pages. The text is Gallican and is accompanied by an explanation of each psalm taken from the Major Glossatura of Peter the Lombard.

St Malachy, on his last journey to the continent in 1148, crossed the Irish Sea from Bangor to the Scottish coast and at Viride Stagnum (Soulscat, Wigtownshire), a place close to where he landed, he founded an abbey. He left some of the monks who had travelled from Ireland with him under the rule of an abbot who was a former monk at Bangor and was probably under the Cistercian rule.

It was here that the Coupar Angus Psalter was written and in spite of its rough decoration and its gaudy colour scheme, there are many similarities with the Corpus Gospels. The scribe's artistic skill was clumsy and inferior, but he may well have studied these manuscripts.

Initial from Coupar Angus Psalter, 12th century

Harley MS 1023
British Library, London

Written at Armagh, this small Gospel Book was produced in 1138 at the same time as the Harley MS 1802 Gospel Book. It has many similar characteristics, including its size of 200 × 142 mm (7⅞" × 5½"), to the Book of Armagh. Only eighty-eight pages remain and the greater part of the Gospel of St Matthew is lost, so we do not know whether it had prefaces and canon-tables. It was written in Irish minuscule by several scribes who inserted glosses and explanations of words, in Irish and Latin, in the borders. The initials are the knotted-wire type with colour panels of yellow, pink, red lead and purple.

Very few manuscripts can be ascribed to the first half of the 12th century – energies were probably devoted to the restoration of the ruined monasteries after the devastation from the Norse invaders in the 10th and 11th centuries. Armagh like many other monasteries at this time focused their efforts on reviving the spirit of scriptorium and traditions of the past.

Initial and symbol of St Mark from Harley MS 1023, 12th century

Harley MS 1802
British Library, London

The Irish schools in the second half of the century began sending their students abroad to centres of learning so that on their return they could study and adapt the new ideas they had learnt. Flann O'Gorman, who was head of the Armagh schools from 1154 to 1174, had himself studied for some time outside Ireland.

This Gospel Book was created at the same time as Harley MS 1023 though it is smaller in size 165 × 121 mm (6½" × 4¾") and has 156 pages. The text is written in a mixture of Irish and Latin in an unbelievably small Irish minuscule which often overflows onto additional sheets of vellum inserted here and there. It was planned from the start that the wide margins, which were very fashionable on the Continent, would take a commentary of the text. Notes written at the end of each Gospel by the scribe Máel Brigte Ua Máeluánaig refer to historical events which gives the document its date of 1138.

The four Gospels are introduced by initials of black interlace with animal heads and colour grounds. The colours used are orange, green, yellow and purple, and the frames are yellow panels enclosing a variety of key and step patterns. For the symbol pages of Mark and Luke to fit, the artist has laid the frames into an upright position. The symbol pages of Matthew and John are missing.

Initial from Harley MS 1802, 12th century

Top: Chi-Rho, 12th century
Bottom: symbol of St Luke from Harley MS 1802, 12th century

Corpus Gospels

MS 122 Corpus Christi College Library, Oxford

This small Gospel Book is similar in size to Harley MS 1023 at 215 × 140 mm (8½" × 5½"). It is nearly complete, lacking only the Gospel of St John. It has been excellently preserved and the vellum has kept its ivory whiteness – the colours are also bright and sharp which gives us a good idea what the earlier manuscripts would have looked like in their original state.

The evidence for the Corpus Gospels being connected with the monastery of Bangor comes from an unusual addition inserted between the canon-tables and the Novem opus preface. It is a fine drawing of a gaming board with its gaming pieces called the Alea Evangelii. We are told this board game was brought back by Dubinnsi, Bishop of Bangor (d. 953), from the English court of King Athelstan. The possible date for the Gospel is 1140.

Initial from the Corpus Gospels, 12th century

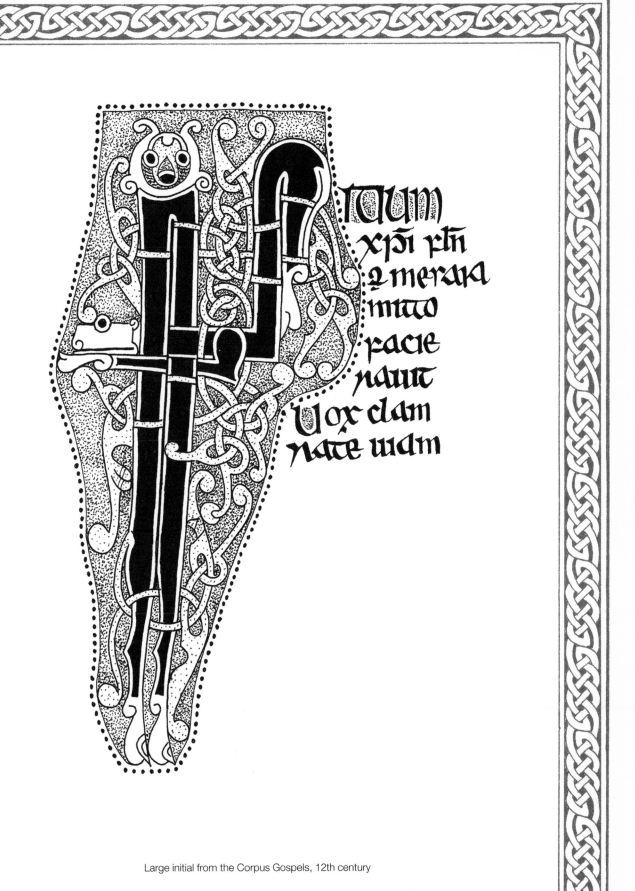

Large initial from the Corpus Gospels, 12th century

Further Reading

Baine, George, *Celtic Art: The Methods of Construction*, London, 1951

Blackhouse, Janet, *The Lindisfarne Gospels*, London, 1981

Brown, Peter, *The Book of Kells*, London, 1980

Carmichael, Alexander, *Carmina Gadelica*, Edinburgh

Davis, Courtney, *The Art of Celtia*, London, 1994

———, *Celtic Art of Courtney Davis*, Saffron Walden, Essex, 1985

———, *The Celtic Art Source Book*, London, 1985

———, *Celtic Borders and Decoration*, London, 1992

———, *Celtic Design and Motifs*, New York, 1991

———, *Celtic Image*, London, 1996

———, *Celtic Initials and Alphabet*, London, 1997

———, *The Celtic Mandala Book*, London, 1993

———, *Celtic Ornament, the Art of the Scribe*, London, 1996

———, *The Celtic Saint Book*, London, 1995

———, *The Celtic Tarot*, London, 1990

———, *The Return of King Arthur*, London, 1995

Gill, Elaine, Everett, David, and Davis,Courtney, *Celtic Pilgrimages*, London, 1997

Henderson, George, *From Durrow to Kells*, London, 1987

Henry, Françoise, *Irish Art in the Romanesque Period*, London, 1970

———, *Irish Art*, London, 1967

Laing, Lloyd and Jennifer, *Art of the Celts*, London, 1992

Meehan, Bernard, *The Book of Kells*, London, 1994

Nordenfalk, Carl, *Celtic and Anglo-Saxon Painting*, London, 1977

Quiller, Peter, and Davis, Courtney, *Merlin Awakes*, London, 1990

———, *Merlin the Immortal*, Reading, 1987

Roberts, Forrester, and Davis, Courtney, *Symbols of the Grail Quest*, St Austell, 1990

Romilly Allen, J., *Celtic Art in Pagan and Christian Times*, London, 1993

Webster Wilde, Lyn, and Davis, Courtney, *Celtic Women*, London, 1997

You can view the work of Courtney Davis on his web site
http://www.wdi.co.uk/celtic

1 Tory
2 Inishmurray
3 Inishbofin
4 Aran
5 Skellig Michael

Irish monastic centres

Index

Acknowledgments

My thanks go to my partner Dimity and to my children Blaine and Bridie for their patience with me while I worked. To Dennis O'Neill for his foreword, to Michael Law who sorts out my Mac every time it crashes, and to my agents Mike and Laura Elliott. Thanks also to Nigel Melville for his help on the text and translation and to the Wheelwrights' tea room – my sanctuary.

Border from the Book of Kells, 9th century

Prayer from St Patrick's Evening Hymn

May the virtue of our daily work
Hallow our nightly prayers.
May our sleep be deep and soft,
So our work be fresh and hard.

Portrait of St John, Macdurnan Gospels, 9th century